# Contents

# ▬ *introduction* ▬
# To the Teacher

### The Course

This course consists of the students' book and cassette tape. It is designed to be used in class or as self-study material. The comprehensive key includes the script of all recorded material not in the individual students' units.

### The Aim

The title Basic Telephone Training speaks for itself. The course is designed to make elementary students efficient telephone users within a limited area. At the end of this course, students should be able to cope with the telephone duties of a secretary or switchboard operator.

### The Structure of the Course

The course is in two parts:

Units 1 – 13: Basic Telephone Language

These units teach the functional phrases and vocabulary necessary. This includes crucial areas such as numbers, dates, and prepositions, where accuracy is essential.

Units 14 – 28: Basic Telephone Skills

1 Listening: the A parts of these units

2 Taking messages: the B parts

3 Speaking: the role play Phone Play sections

### Teaching the Course

You can work through the course unit by unit or you can alternate units from the second part with units from the first. Lower level students should not start Part 2 until they have completed most if not all of Part 1.

### Role-play Phone Plays

These are information-gap pair work exercises. It is excellent if students can use telephones and sit in different rooms. If this is impossible, ask students to sit in pairs, back to back, and perform the Phone Plays without looking at each other.

# Basic Telephone Training

A Basic Course in Telephone Language Skills

## Anne Watson-Delestrée

THOMSON

HEINLE

Australia Canada Mexico Singapore Spain United Kingdom United Sta.

**Basic Telephone Training**
*Anne Watson-Delestrée*

**Publisher/Global ELT:** *Christopher Wenger*
**Executive Marketing Manager/Global ELT/ESL:** *Amy Mabley*

Printed in the UK
    6 7 8 9 10  06 05 04 03 02

For more information contact Heinle, 25 Thomson Place, Boston, MA 02210 USA,
or you can visit our Internet site at http://www.heinle.com

**ISBN:** 0-906717-42-6

**The Author**
Anne Watson-Delestrée is a British teacher of English, living and working in Paris. She has long experience of ESP teaching. She developed this course for the many hundreds of students she taught who needed to use and understand English on the telephone. In its initial form she used this course successfully in many schools and companies in the Paris area. She is grateful for the comments of all her colleagues over the years who trialled the material and offered suggestions. In particular, she thanks Anne Pichon for her help, and colleagues at A.V.L. and Bull, Paris, for piloting several units.

**Acknowledgements**
Cover design and illustrations by Anna Macleod
Cover photograph courtesy of Zefa

# To the Student

### Speaking on the Telephone

Learning to speak a new language is difficult. Learning to speak it on the telephone – when you cannot see the caller – is even more difficult. This course teaches you to listen, to speak, and to take messages.

### The Dialogues

All the dialogues are on tape. Listen to them once or twice, sometimes looking at your book, sometimes just listening. When you repeat after the tape, try not to look at your book. Do this several times until you sound natural. Then read the dialogue aloud without the tape.

### Different Accents

The tape has different accents: American, Scottish, Australian etc. When you use the telephone at work, everyone has a different accent!

### The Exercises

All the answers to the exercises are in the self-study Key at the end of the book. Try to do an exercise without looking at the key. If you find an exercise difficult, look at the key, but close the Key before you write the answers.

### Learning at Home

If you are studying this course at home without a teacher, here is some advice specially for you:

1 Do not be afraid to use the Key – the Key is your teacher.

2 Do not try to go too fast. Finish one unit before starting the next. Make sure you understand everything in one unit before you begin the next.

3 Try to do some of the units from the Basic Telephone Skills part while you are studying units 1-13.

4 Decide a timetable for studying and stick to it!

# Starting the Call

*1* Listen to this conversation. Repeat after the tape.

You **CPA Corporation. Good morning.**

Caller **Hello. I'd like to speak to Mr Martin, please.**

You **Who's speaking, please?**

Caller **This is John Bush of Lion Computers.**

You **Hold the line, please. I'll put you through . . .**

**. . . Go ahead, Mr Bush. You're through.**

*Tip* Don't just answer *Hello!* Give your name.

*2* Here are other phrases you can use. Put them in the correct order to make a conversation. Then read them aloud.

| | | | |
|---|---|---|---|
| A | Can I speak to Mr Martin, please? | 1 | |
| B | One moment, please. I'm putting you through. | 2 | |
| C | John Bush of Lion Computers. | 3 | |
| D | Accounts Department. Can I help you? | 4 | |
| E | Who's calling? | 5 | |

Now listen to this dialogue on tape.

*3* Fill in the spaces in this conversation – for *your* firm:

You .................. Good morning.

Caller Can I speak to ................. , please?

You .................. , please. ....................

*4* Listen to the tape. Fill in the spaces in these conversations:

a You Interface ................... . Can I help you?

Caller Hello. ......... I speak to Mr Stevenson, please?

You ......... moment, please. I'm ................... .

b You      PLC International. .................... .

Caller      .................... speak to Mr Davies, please.

You      Who's ...................., please?

Caller      .................... Charles Windsor of Micro Logics.

You      .................... , please. I'll .................... .

5    Write expressions which mean the same. The first one is done for you.

Belfry Consultants. Can I
help you?

*Good morning, Belfry Consultants.*

I'd like to speak to Mr Brown,
please.

........................................

Who's speaking, please?

........................................

This is Brian Howard of Jason's.

........................................

Hold on, Mr Howard. ................

I'll connect you. ........................ .

6    Look at this telephone number from Britain to Hungary.

| 010 36 | 1 | 44 69 32 |
|---|---|---|
| international code | area code | phone number |

Look in your own telephone directory. What are the international codes from *your* country for the following:

1 Australia ..................

3 New Zealand ..................

2 India ..................

4 Algeria ..................

What are the area codes for the following cities:

5 Edinburgh ..................

7 Manchester ..................

6 Washington ..................

8 Sydney ..................

7

# unit 2
# The Boss is Out

**1**    Listen to this conversation. Repeat after the tape.

| | |
|---|---|
| You | **Digital Electronics. Good afternoon.** |
| Caller | **Can I speak to Mr Burton, please?** |
| You | **I'm sorry, but Mr Burton is in a meeting. Can I take a message?** |
| Caller | **No, it's all right. What time will he be free?** |
| You | **At 3 o'clock.** |
| Caller | **Could you tell him I called – it's Mr Rees.** |
| You | **Certainly.** |
| Caller | **Thanks very much. Goodbye.** |
| You | **Goodbye.** |

*Tip*    *Certainly* means *yes* and is very friendly.

**2**    Here are other phrases you can use. Put the lines in the correct order to make a conversation. Then read them aloud.

| | | |
|---|---|---|
| A | No, it's alright. When will she be back? | |
| B | Certainly Mr Blair. | |
| C | Walker and Williams. Good morning. | |
| D | Thanks for your help. | |
| E | Please tell her I called. | |
| F | I'm sorry she's out at the moment. | |
| G | You're welcome. Goodbye. | |
| H | Can I speak to Mrs Blair, please. I'm Mr Blair. | |
| I | I'm afraid I don't know. | |

| |   |
|---|---|
| 1 | |
| 2 | |
| 3 | |
| 4 | |
| 5 | |
| 6 | |
| 7 | |
| 8 | |
| 9 | |

*Tip*    In this conversation *I'm afraid* = I'm sorry. Use *I'm afraid* to give bad or negative information.

**3**    Listen to the tape. Fill in the spaces in these conversations:

a
| | |
|---|---|
| You | I'm .................. Mr Jones is .................. . |
| Caller | Oh dear. .................. will he be .................. ? |
| You | At about .................. . |
| Caller | Well, could you .................. , please? |

8

b You    Hello. I'm ..................... but Gloria is..................... .

Can I ..................... ?

Caller    No, that's all right. Could you just ................... ?

4 This conversation is 'foreign'. Re-write it so that it sounds more natural and friendly.

| | | |
|---|---|---|
| You | Hello. José Vidal here. | *Good morning, José Vidal speaking.*..... |
| Caller | Mrs Rossi, please. | ............................................... |
| You | Mrs Rossi's not here. You call back? | ............................................... ............................................... |
| Caller | What time? | ............................................... |
| You | 20 minutes. | ............................................... |
| Caller | Thank you. | ............................................... |
| You | It's OK. | ............................................... |

*Tip*    Did you notice that you *added* extra phrases to make the information sound better?

5 Listen to the tape. Fill in the correct day of the week in the following sentences:

   1    He won't be back till .................. .

   2    We open again on .................. morning at 9.

   3    We shall be closed from .................. the 16th until .................. the 18th.

   4    The best time to ring is before lunch on .................. or after 5pm on .................. .

6 Look at this calendar. Today is the 16th. Write the dates in the spaces:

| M | Tu | W | Th | F | Sa | Su |
|---|---|---|---|---|---|---|
| 1 | 2 | 3 | 4 | 5 | 6 | 7 |
| 8 | 9 | 10 | 11 | 12 | 13 | 14 |
| 15 | (16) | 17 | 18 | 19 | 20 | 21 |
| 22 | 23 | 24 | 25 | 26 | 27 | 28 |
| 29 | 30 | 31 | | | | |

   1   today ............     2   tomorrow ............     3   yesterday ............

   4   a week today ............     5   a week tomorrow ............

   6   last Tuesday............     7   a fortnight tomorrow ............

*Tip*    Don't say 7/8 days or 14/15 days in English. Say a *week* or a *fortnight*.

# unit 3
# The Wrong Number

**1**   The wrong company. Listen to this conversation. Repeat after the tape.

> **You**      **420 976**
>
> **Caller**   **Can I speak to Mr Rose, please?**
>
> **You**      **I'm sorry there's nobody of that name here. I think you've got the wrong number.**
>
> **Caller**   **I'm sorry to have bothered you. Goodbye.**
>
> **You**      **Goodbye.**

*Tip*   Note that you said *I think you've got the wrong number*. This sounds better than *You've got the wrong number*, which sounds aggressive.

**2**   Here are other phrases you can use. Put the lines in the correct order to make a conversation. Then read them aloud.

> A      553 976
>
> B      Oh, I'm very sorry I must have the wrong number. Cheerio.
>
> C      Is that 553 956?
>
> D      Cheerio.
>
> E      No, this is 553 976.

| | |
|---|---|
| 1 | |
| 2 | |
| 3 | |
| 4 | |
| 5 | |

**3**   Fill in the spaces with information about *yourself:*

> a  **Caller**   Is that Tell Brothers?
>
>    **You**      No, this .................... .
>
> b  **Caller**   I'd like to speak to Miss Van Hertzen, please.
>
>    **You**      I'm sorry there's .................... .
>
> c  **Caller**   Is that 489 9929?
>
>    **You**      No, .................... .

*4*   The wrong department. Listen to this conversation. Then fill in the spaces:

   You      Susan McQueen speaking. Good afternoon.

   Caller   Is .................... extension 584?

   You      No, this is 554. I'll put you .................... to the switchboard.

   Caller   Thanks for your help.

   You      That's all right. Goodbye.


*5*   Look at the information. Listen to the tape. Write your reply.

   1      (Your name is Dorothy Smith.)

          ......................................................................................................................

   2      (Your number is 992 4097.)

          ......................................................................................................................

   3      (Your name is Mr Reynolds.)

          ......................................................................................................................


*6*   Put this conversation in the correct order. The first line is correct.

   A Caller   Could I speak to Mary Stone, please?

   B You      No, this is extension 1245. Which department
              is she in?

   C Caller   Thanks for your help. I'm sorry to have
              bothered you. Goodbye.

   D You      I'll put you through to her department.

   E Caller   Training.

   F You      That's all right. Goodbye.

   G Caller   Oh! Isn't that extension 1235?

   H You      There's nobody of that name here, I'm afraid.

| | |
|---|---|
| 1 | A |
| 2 | |
| 3 | |
| 4 | |
| 5 | |
| 6 | |
| 7 | |
| 8 | |

# ▬ *unit 4* ▬
# **A** Bad Line

1    Listen to this conversation. Repeat the phrases after the tape.

| | |
|---|---|
| You | **The Bank of Scotland. Good afternoon.** |
| Caller | **This is .....................** |
| You | **Sorry?** |
| Caller | **This is .....................** |
| You | **I'm sorry, but the line is very bad. Please speak up.** |
| Caller | **This is the Accounts Department of .....................** |
| You | **I'm sorry, but I still can't hear you. This line is very bad. Could you please ring back.** |

2    Practise saying these phrases after the tape:

a    When you can't hear:

**Sorry?**
**Pardon?**
**I can't hear you. The line is very bad.**
**Please speak up.**

b    When you don't understand:

**I'm sorry, but I don't understand.**
**Sorry, but I still don't understand.**
**Please speak more slowly.**

c    When you are not sure:

**Could you repeat that, please.**
**Could you spell that, please.**
**Please confirm by fax.**

*Tip*    Use *sorry* on the phone when you have a problem of some kind – you don't understand or you can't hear.

3  Listen to the tape. Fill in the spaces in this conversation:

Caller   This is Paul Down speaking.

You      ................... ?

Caller   Paul Down speaking.

You      ................... but the line is very bad.

Caller   PAUL DOWN.

You      Could you ................... that, ................... .

Caller   P.A.U.L. D.O.W.N.

You      Could you ................... that, please.

Caller   P..A..U..L.. D..O..W..N

You      ................... , but I ................... don't understand.

Caller   P..A..U..

You      Ah! Good afternoon, Mr Down. How are you?


4  Fill in this puzzle.

1   Sorry? or ................... ?            _ _ _ |D| _ _

2   You're speaking too quickly.
    Please speak more ...................      _ _ |O| _ _ _

3   I don't ...................                _ |N| _ _ _ _ _ _ _

4   I ................... don't understand.    _ |T| _ _


5   Speak more loudly. Please
    speak ...................                  _ |P|

6   Say that again. Could you
    ................... that, please?          _ _ _ _ |A| _

7   I don't speak ...................
    very well.                                _ |N| _ _ _ _ _

8   The ................... is very bad.
    I can't hear you.                         _ |I| _ _

9   Please ................... by fax.         |C| _ _ _ _ _ _

13

# unit 5
# **A**nswering Machines

*1*  Here are 5 different messages. Listen to each one on tape. Then read it aloud. Then record it yourself on a blank cassette.

a  General information – no tone

**This is All Africa Export Ltd. Our office is closed at the moment. We're open from 9 am to 6 pm – Monday to Friday. Thank you for calling.**

b  Office closed – with tone

**This is Duquesnes International. Our office is closed at the moment. Please leave your name and phone number and we'll call you back when we open. Speak after the tone.**

c  'Holding' message – no tone

**Thank you for calling Transglobal Airways. Your call is in a queue. Please hold on until one of our agents is free. We're sorry to keep you waiting . . . .**

d  More informal message – with tone

**This is John Bach's office. I'm not in at the moment, but I'll call you back when I return. Please leave your name and number after the tone. Thanks for ringing.**

e  Message to fax – no tone

**This is Agri-Cultura. The office is on holiday for two weeks. We re-open on Monday the 18th. If you have an urgent message, you may fax us on 26 28 70 – that's fax number 26 28 70.**

*2*  Look again at these messages. Write any useful phrases in the space below – phrases you think you can use.

.................................................................................................................

.................................................................................................................

.................................................................................................................

.................................................................................................................

*3*  Write 3 messages. Use *your* name and/or the name of *your* company.

1  You're going to a meeting and won't be back in the office till tomorrow.

........................................................................................

........................................................................................

........................................................................................

2  It's 6 o'clock. You're going home.

........................................................................................

........................................................................................

........................................................................................

3  Your office is closing at lunchtime today. Business as usual tomorrow.

........................................................................................

........................................................................................

........................................................................................

*4*  Listen to the tape. Fill in the spaces in these messages.

1  .................... LTP. Please .................... .

   We're sorry to ........................................ .

2  This is Henry Barber's office. I'm .................... right now, but if you

   leave me .................... and your phone number, I'll .................... when

   I return. Please speak .................... .

# Number Revision

*1*    Make sure you can say all these numbers.

0  1  2  3  4  5  6  7  8  9  10

11  12  13  14  15  16  17  18  19  20

21  22  23

30  40  50  60  70  80  90  100

101 – a hundred and one    111 – a hundred and eleven

1000 – a thousand    100,000 – a hundred thousand

1,000,000 – a million

*2*    Look at these examples. Say them after the tape.

| | |
|---|---|
| 78 | seventy-eight |
| 425 | four hundred and twenty-five |
| 1210 | one thousand, two hundred and ten |
| 48601 | forty-eight thousand, six hundred and one |
| 939837 | nine hundred and thirty-nine thousand, eight hundred and thirty-seven |

*3*    Write these numbers in words.

1    51   .........................................................................

2    812   .........................................................................

3    4739   .........................................................................

4    204110   .........................................................................

**4** Write in figures.

1 twenty-eight thousand nine hundred and fourteen ...............

2 seven hundred and four ...............

3 two thousand three hundred and fifty-one ...............

4 six hundred and thirty-four thousand four hundred and five ...............

**5** Listen to the tape and fill in this puzzle.

17

# Telephone Numbers

*1*    Listen to these dialogues, then repeat them after the tape.

    a  Caller    **. . . Could you give me Mr Hansen's home number, please?**

        You    **Yes, it's a different code – oh..two..nine..three –
five..nine..oh..double six..three.**

        Caller    **0293 – 590 663.**

        You    **That's right.**

    b  You    **Baker and Williams. Good morning.**

        Caller    **Could I have extension 132, please.**

        You    **Who's calling?**

        Caller    **Helen de Witt.**

        You    **One moment, please. I'll put you through.**

*Tips*

Say numbers separately.
Say *three..seven..four.*

Pause between groups.
Say 325....651.
Say 89...44...90

Say *oh* for 0. It is better
than zero or naught.

For 66, say *double 6.*
for 666, say *six, double six.*

For 4981 Ext 242, say:
*four..nine..eight..one –
extension two four two.*

For 0456-62321, the *area code*
is 0456 and the *number* is 62321.

*2*    Listen to the tape and correct these numbers:

    1    031 456 9567   .................................................................

    2    22 31 49 02   .................................................................

    3    69 60 51 333   .................................................................

    4    236 02 84   .................................................................

*3*  Listen to the tape and fill in these numbers:

## OFFICE DIRECTORY

| | |
|---|---|
| Brown, George | |
| Bunter, Philip | |
| Carlsson, Sven | |
| Davidson, Julie | |
| Ford, Ellen | |
| Hindley, Paul | |

*4*  Listen and add the phone numbers:

## EUROPEAN SALES OFFICES

| | |
|---|---|
| Amsterdam | |
| Brussels | |
| Copenhagen | |
| Dublin | |
| Frankfurt | |
| Helsinki | |

# unit 8
# The Date

*1*    Say the year in pairs. Look at these examples.

|      |          |                       |
|------|----------|-----------------------|
| 1993 | 19 . . . 93 | nineteen ninety-three |
| 1901 | 19 . . . 01 | nineteen oh-one       |
| 1978 | 19 . . . 78 | nineteen seventy-eight |

*2*    When were they born? Listen and fill in the years.

| | |
|---|---|
| Marie Curie | |
| Harpo Marx | |
| Graham Greene | |
| J. F. Kennedy | |
| Grace Kelly | |
| Prince Edward | |

*3*    Use ordinal numbers for dates. Practise saying these.

| | | | | | |
|---|---|---|---|---|---|
| 1st | the first | 11th | the eleventh | 22nd | the twenty-second |
| 2nd | the second | 12th | the twelfth | 23rd | the twenty-third |
| 3rd | the third | 13th | the thirteenth | 24th | the twenty-fourth |
| 4th | the fourth | 14th | the fourteenth | 25th | the twenty-fifth |
| 5th | the fifth | 15th | the fifteenth | 26th | the twenty-sixth |
| 6th | the sixth | 16th | the sixteenth | 27th | the twenty-seventh |
| 7th | the seventh | 17th | the seventeenth | 28th | the twenty-eighth |
| 8th | the eighth | 18th | the eighteenth | 29th | the twenty-ninth |
| 9th | the ninth | 19th | the nineteenth | 30th | the thirtieth |
| 10th | the tenth | 20th | the twentieth | 31st | the thirty-first |
| | | 21st | the twenty-first | | |

*4*    Right (✔) or wrong (✗)? Listen to the tape and correct if necessary.

| | | |
|---|---|---|
| 1 | 13th | |
| 2 | 31st | |
| 3 | 12th | |
| 4 | 9th | |
| 5 | 15th | |
| 6 | 11th | |

**5**   Look at this calendar. Practise reading the dates.

| May | | | | | | |
|---|---|---|---|---|---|---|
| 1 | 2 | 3 | 4 | 5 | 6 | 7 |
| 8 | 9 | 10 | 11 | 12 | 13 | 14 |
| 15 | 16 | (17) | 18 | 19 | 20 | 21 |
| 22 | 23 | 24 | 25 | 26 | 27 | 28 |
| 29 | 30 | 31 | | | | |

GB   Write   17th May 1994
        or      (17/5/94)
        Say    the seventeenth of May, nineteen ninety-four
        or      May the seventeenth
USA  Write  May 17, 1994
        or      (5/17/94)
        Say    May seventeenth, nineteen ninety-four

**6**   Write these dates.

1  GB  The eighth of June, nineteen ninety-four .............................

2  US  September sixteenth, nineteen eighty .............................

3  GB  The eleventh of October, nineteen sixty-three .............................

4  US  July thirty-first, nineteen thirty-nine .............................

5  GB  ................................................................ 6/8/91

6  US  ................................................................ 6/8/91

7  GB  ................................................................ 20/10/94

8  US  ................................................................ 12/14/96

**7**   Listen to the tape and fill in the dates on Betty's list of things to do.

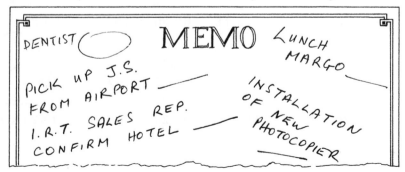

21

# Telling the Time

There are two ways of saying the time.

## 1  The Digital System – It's ten forty-five.

Look at these examples. Listen and repeat after the tape:

| | |
|---|---|
| a | 6.30 in the morning |
| b | 2.45 in the afternoon |
| c | 7.00 in the evening |
| d | 11.20 at night |

When looking at a timetable, the 24 hour digital system is used:

| | |
|---|---|
| e | 13.05 = thirteen oh five |
| f | 19.55 = nineteen fifty five |
| g | 21.10 = twenty-one ten |

*Tip*  Say *am* before 12 midday (12.00) and *pm* from midday until midnight (00.00)

## 2  The Classical System – It's a quarter to eleven

Look at these examples. Listen and repeat after the tape.

**It's 8 o'clock.   It's half past 8.   It's a quarter past 8.   It's a quarter to 8.**

**It's 5 past 8.   It's 10 past 8.   It's 20 past 8.       It's 25 past 8.**

**It's 5 to 4.       It's 10 to 4.       It's 20 to 4.       It's 25 to 4.**

*Tip*  Ask the questions: *What's the time?* or *What time is it?* or if your watch or clock has stopped – *What time do you make it?*

*3*  Change to classical time.

    1  12.05    ...........................................................................................

    2  14.25    ...........................................................................................

    3  10.40    ...........................................................................................

    4  20.55    ...........................................................................................


*4*  Change to digital time.

    1  a quarter to nine in the evening        .............................................

    2  10 past 10 in the morning               .............................................

    3  5 to 1 in the morning                   .............................................

    4  25 past 11 at night                     .............................................


*5*  Listen to the tape. Fill in the information on this cinema timetable.


## REX CINEMA

| 1 | 2 | 3 | 4 | 5 |
|---|---|---|---|---|
| MAD MAX XI | ROCKY XV | TERMINATOR VII | RAMBO XX | HENRY V |
|  |  |  |  |  |

# **S**pelling Clearly

*1*   Repeat these letters after the tape.

| | 1 | 2 | 3 | 4 | 5 | 6 | 7 |
|---|---|---|---|---|---|---|---|
| | (pay)<br>( ɛI ) | (see)<br>( i: ) | (left)<br>( ɛ ) | (eye)<br>( aI ) | (go)<br>(əʊ) | (queue)<br>( u: ) | (bar)<br>( ɑ: ) |
| | a | b | f | i | o | q | r |
| | h | c | l | y | | u | |
| | j | d | m | | | w | |
| | k | e | n | | | | |
| | | g | s | | | | |
| | | p | x | | | | |
| | | t | z - GB | | | | |
| | | v | | | | | |
| | | z - US | | | | | |

z – GB = ZED    z – US = ZEE

*2*   Practise spelling. Listen and repeat after the tape.

   ROAD    LANE    STREET    WAY    CLOSE

*Tip*   For EE, say *double E* or *E..E*

*3*   Use this International Spelling Alphabet as a guide:

**A as in Amsterdam**

| | | |
|---|---|---|
| A – Amsterdam | J – Jerusalem | S – Santiago |
| B – Baltimore | K – Kilogram | T – Tripoli |
| C – Casablanca | L – Liverpool | U – Uppsala |
| D – Denmark | M – Madagascar | V – Valencia |
| E – Edison | N – New York | W – Washington |
| F – Florida | O – Oslo | X – X-ray |
| G – Gallipoli | P – Paris | Y – Yokohama |
| H – Havana | Q – Quebec | Z – Zürich |
| I – Italy | R – Roma | |

**4**  Invent your own spelling guide with words you know.

**For example: A – apple   B – BBC**

| | | | | | |
|---|---|---|---|---|---|
| A | .......................... | J | .......................... | S | .......................... |
| B | .......................... | K | .......................... | T | .......................... |
| C | .......................... | L | .......................... | U | .......................... |
| D | .......................... | M | .......................... | V | .......................... |
| E | .......................... | N | .......................... | W | .......................... |
| F | .......................... | O | .......................... | X | .......................... |
| G | .......................... | P | .......................... | Y | .......................... |
| H | .......................... | Q | .......................... | Z | .......................... |
| I | .......................... | R | .......................... | | |

**5**  Listen to the tape and fill in these application forms:

1
Family Name:

Forename(s):

Place of Birth:

2
Family Name:

Forename(s):

Place of Birth:

3
Family Name:

Forename(s):

Place of Birth:

4
Family Name:

Forename(s):

Place of Birth:

# unit 11
# Taking an Address

*1*  Listen to this dialogue. Repeat after the tape.

| | |
|---|---|
| You | **Could you give me the address, please.** |
| Caller | **Certainly, are you ready?** |
| You | **Go ahead.** |
| Caller | **Quimica Colombia...that's Quimica..new word Colombia. Avenida Villa Neuva 17A23/45...that's Avenida..new word..Villa..new word..Neuva..new word..17..capital A..23..stroke..45 ..new line..Bogota..new line..Colombia.** |
| You | **Could you spell Quimica, please?** |
| Caller | **Q as in queen, U as in umbrella, I as in India, M as in mother, I as in India, C as in cat, A as in apple.** |
| You | **Thank you very much. Goodbye.** |
| Caller | **Goodbye.** |

*Tip*  Spell difficult words with your spelling guide.

*2*  Say these important words after the tape:

    1 .  full stop (or stop)
    2 -  hyphen
    3 –  dash
    4 /  stroke (UK) slash (US)
    5 ABC in capitals (or capital A, capital B, capital C)
    6 abc small letters
    7 PVa capital P, capital V, small a
    8 new word
    9 new line
    10 postcode – zipcode

*3*  Look at this address. Listen to it on tape, then repeat it.

  D-V-H Nederland B.V.
  Zeedijk 12
  Postbus 409
  1181 VT Amstelveen

Now try to write it out in the same way you would say it on the phone:

...............................................................................................................

...............................................................................................................

*Tip*  Postcode is British English; zipcode is American English.

**4**    Listen to the tape and write in the new addresses on these cards.

---

**1**

Please note that
**Workwell Watches**
**Bahnhofstrasse 78**
**8021 ZURICH**

is moving to

_____

_____

on 23rd January

---

**2**

_Our new address as from 10th March will be_

_____

_____

# The Goya Art Gallery

Marques de Valdeiglesias 15
Madrid 4

---

**3**

## CHANGE OF ADDRESS
AS OF 13th OCTOBER

Pyramid Sandpapers Ltd             **Pyramid Sandpapers Ltd**

28 Kulliyet El Ziraa Street         _____

PO BOX 190                          _____

Cairo                               _____

# ◼ *unit 12* ◼
# **P**repositions

*1*  Look at these prepositions of time:

| ON Monday, Thursday . . .<br>the 12th (of July) . . .<br>**Christmas Day**<br>**New Year's Day** | IN January, March . . .<br><br>summer, winter . . .<br><br>1993 . . . | AT 10 o'clock . . .<br><br>the weekend<br><br>night |
|---|---|---|
| **BY Friday . . .**<br>**20th June . . .**<br>**next week . . .** | the morning<br><br>the afternoon<br><br>the evening | noon, midday<br><br>midnight<br><br>Christmas |
| **UNTIL Wednesday . . .**<br>**the 11th . . .**<br>**next month . . .** | half an hour . . .<br><br>20 minutes . . . | Easter |

*2*  When was the accident? Fill in the time with the correct preposition.

1. It was  ......................

2. It was  ......................

3. It was ......................

4. It was  ......................

5. It was  ......................

6. It was ......................

*3*  Study these prepositions of place.

| AT a meeting, conference<br>the airport, station<br>the restaurant<br>the office, work<br>IBM<br>home | IN Spain, the USA . . .<br>London, Berlin . . .<br>the office (inside)<br>hospital | ON holiday<br>vacation<br>a business trip<br>a mission<br>a special project |
|---|---|---|

*Tip*  After a verb of movement, use *to* with all places except *home*: He drives *to* the office. I flew *to* Belgium. They're going *to* the pub. We went home.

28

**4**   Where's Mr Horimoto? Fill in the preposition:

1. He's ..... work.   2. He's ..... lunch.   3. He's ..... a business trip.

4. He's ..... holiday.   5. He's ...... a meeting.   6. He's ..... New York.

**5**   Fill in the spaces with a preposition:

1   Please ask Mr Smith to meet me ................... Victoria Station ................... 3rd May ................... 11 o'clock.

2   Terry is................... Mexico ................... a business trip ................... the silver factory this week.

3   Our phone rings more ................... the morning than ................... the afternoon and never ................... the evening.

4   I'll be ................... my office or ................... the conference ................... Wednesday when you arrive.

5   The company will be closed ................... August and ................... Christmas.

6   I'm coming ................... Tokyo ................... Friday and staying ................... Tuesday.

7   Please finish this project ................... the end of the month.

8   Mr Brown's secretary is going ................... the bank before she goes ................... home.

**6**   Fill in the prepositions:

| 1   ............ | night | 2   ............ | the morning |
|---|---|---|---|
| | work | | Australia |
| | New Year | | February |
| | a conference | | |
| | | 4   ............ | 3 o'clock |
| 3   ............ | Wednesday | | the weekend |
| | the 1st of June | | home |
| | holiday | | noon |
| | a business trip | | the dentist |

*29*

# Basic Language Revision

This unit revises the most important language in units 1-12.

1 Fill in one word in each space in these conversations:

a You     Rapide Communications. Good morning.

Caller    Good morning. Could I speak to Mr Davidson, ..........?

You      .......... . .......... I have your name, ..........?

Caller    Manfred Schwarz from Hamburg.

You      .......... the line, Mr Schwarz.

b You     Mr Davidson's secretary. How can I help you?

Caller    I'd like to speak to Mr Davidson, please.

You      .......... Mr Davidson is .......... holiday this week.
.......... you like to leave a ..........?

Caller    Yes, could you ask him to give me a ring when he gets back. My name is Sussman.

You      Could you .......... that, ..........?

Caller    It's S..U.............S..M..A..N.

You      Thank you, Mr Sussman, I'll leave a note for him.

c You     Extension 230.

Caller    Oh, I'm sorry. I asked for extension 320.

You      Hold .........., please. I'll .......... you back to the .......... .

2 Match up the phrase on the left with the phrase on the right which means the same:

| | |
|---|---|
| 1 Hold on. | A Goodbye |
| 2 I'd like to . . . | B Pardon? |
| 3 I'll put you through. | C Connect |
| 4 Yes. | D Call |
| 5 I'm sorry . . . | E Who's calling? |
| 6 Cheerio. | F Can I . . . |
| 7 Sorry? | G Hold the line. |
| 8 Ring. | H I'm afraid . . . |
| 9 Who's speaking? | I I'll connect you. |
| 10 Put through. | J Certainly. |

| | |
|---|---|
| 1 | G |
| 2 | |
| 3 | |
| 4 | |
| 5 | |
| 6 | |
| 7 | |
| 8 | |
| 9 | |
| 10 | |

**3**     When you make an international call:

       First you dial the ......... ......... .

       Then you dial the ......... ......... .

       Then you dial the number.

**4**     Fill in the spaces in these recorded messages – one word in each space:

    1   Thank you for ......... Godfrey Smith Associates. I'm sorry there's

       ......... here to answer your call. If you ......... your name and

       telephone number after the ......... , we'll ring you back as ......... as

       we can.

    2   CPA Ltd. All lines are engaged at present. Your ......... is in a queue.

       Please hold ......... and your call will be answered shortly.

    3   Mediterranean Tours. Our office is now ......... for the day. Our office

       hours are from 9.30 ......... till 5.30 ......... . If you ......... like us to call

       you ......... , please leave your name and number after the tone.

**5**     Put this conversation in the correct order:

| | |
|---|---|
| A   I'm sorry, but he's at a meeting. Could I take a message? | 1 |
| B   Certainly. I'll let him know. | 2 |
| C   Goodbye. | 3 |
| D   Music International. Good afternoon. | 4 |
| E   Certainly. Thank you for ringing. | 5 |
| F   Good afternoon. This is Mr Bellamy's travel agent. | 6 |
| G   Could you also tell him I'll put his tickets in the post today. | 7 |
| H   Yes, of course. Could you tell him his flight to Los Angeles on the 13th has been changed. The departure time is now 9.30 am and not 10.30 am. | 8 |

**6**    Look at this address, then fill in the spaces below:

New Style Woollens
Dept KK5/BAF
205 Bradford Road
Bingley
BD97 5PF

New Style Woollens   that's three words   New   Style   Woollens
Department KK5/BAF   that's ..........K ..........K   5 .......... ..........B
.......... A .......... F  new .......... two .......... five  Bradford Road
new.......... Bingley  I'll .......... that   B..I..N..G..L..E..Y   new .......... and
then the postal code is BD  97  5  PF.

**7**    Here are some of the most important phrases from units 1-12. Only the first
part is given. Can you complete them:

1  Can I speak to Mr Martin .................... .
2  Who's .................... ?
3  One .................... .
4  I'll put you .................... .
5  Can I take a .................... ?
6  Could you tell her I .......... ?
7  I'm sorry there's nobody of .................... .
8  I'm sorry to have .................... .
9  I'm very sorry I must have the .................... .
10 Please confirm by .................... .
11 I'm sorry the line is very .................... .
12 Please speak .................... !
13 You're speaking too fast. Please speak .................... .
14 Please leave your name and number after the .................... .

**8**    Fill in a preposition in each of the following phrases:

| | | | |
|---|---|---|---|
| 1 | ......... the morning | 11 | ......... the tone |
| 2 | ......... the afternoon | 12 | ......... 3 o'clock |
| 3 | ......... the evening | 13 | ......... Thursday |
| 4 | ......... night | 14 | ......... 9 am ......... 6 pm |
| 5 | ......... the phone | 15 | ......... May 1st |
| 6 | ......... the line | 16 | ......... a business trip |
| 7 | ......... holiday | 17 | ......... Friday afternoon |
| 8 | ......... or ......... a meeting | 18 | ......... lunch |
| 9 | ......... home | 19 | ......... work |
| 10 | ......... another line | 20 | the code ......... Berlin |

# ■ *unit 14a* ■
# **L**istening Practice

*1*  Write the numbers you hear on the tape:

1  .....................................  4  .....................................

2  .....................................  5  .....................................

3  .....................................

*2*  Write the letters you hear:

1  .....................................  4  .....................................

2  .....................................  5  .....................................

3  .....................................

*3*  Write the flight numbers from the tape:

1  .....................................  4  .....................................

2  .....................................  5  .....................................

3  .....................................

*4*  Write the letters you hear:

1  .....................................  4  .....................................

2  .....................................  5  .....................................

3  .....................................

## *Phone Play   Student A*

Call Student B. Ask to speak to Mr Smith.

# Getting the Message

Listen to the message on the tape. Make a note of the important information.

*Tip*   Make sure you write down the important details. You don't need to write down every word.

---

TO ................................... DATE .........................

FROM ................................... TIME .........................

MESSAGE

................................................................

................................................................

................................................................

................................................................

................................................................

................................................................

................................................................

MESSAGE TAKEN BY ...................................

---

## *Phone Play   Student B*

Student A will call you. Ask his name.
Connect him to Mr Smith.

# Listening Practice

*1*    Write the numbers you hear on the tape:

1 ..................................................    4 ..................................................

2 ..................................................    5 ..................................................

3 ..................................................

*2*    Circle the correct letter.

1   B   G   D   V      4   X   F   M   S

2   E   P   C   T      5   Z   N   F   X

3   I   Q   U   Y

*3*    Write the year:

1 ..................................................    4 ..................................................

2 ..................................................    5 ..................................................

3 ..................................................

*4*    Punctuation. Write down exactly what you hear.

1 ..................................................    3 ..................................................

2 ..................................................

---

## *Phone Play*   *Student A*

**Call Student B. Ask to speak to Mr Wilson.**

# **G**etting the Message

Listen to the tape and note down the important information.

*Tip*     Remember to write down only the important details.

To ................................... Date .....................

From ................................. Time .....................

Message

.........................................................................

.........................................................................

.........................................................................

.........................................................................

.........................................................................

.........................................................................

.........................................................................

Message taken by .............................................

---

## *Phone Play   Student B*

Student A will call you. Ask for his name.
Mr Wilson is out until 4 o'clock.

# Listening Practice

*1*    Write the letters you hear on the tape:

1 ................................................    4 ................................................

2 ................................................    5 ................................................

3 ................................................

*2*    Write the telephone numbers on the tape:

1 ................................................    4 ................................................

2 ................................................    5 ................................................

3 ................................................

*3*    Fill in the missing letters:

1    k _ d e        4    x z b _

2    b _ l x        5    p r _ i

3    _ o g f

*4*    Circle the correct number you hear on the tape:

1    80    18        4    15    60

2    70    17        5    30    13

3    16    60

## *Phone Play  Student A*

Call Student B. Give your name. Ask to speak to Mrs Taylor. You have a meeting at 3 o'clock.

# Getting the Message

Listen to the tape and note down the important information.

```
┌─────────────────────────────────────────────────────────┐
│                                                           │
│   TO  .........................   DATE  .................  │
│   FROM  .......................   TIME  .................  │
│                                                           │
│   MESSAGE                                                 │
│                                                           │
│   ...................................................     │
│   ...................................................     │
│   ...................................................     │
│   ...................................................     │
│   ...................................................     │
│   ...................................................     │
│   ...................................................     │
│                                                           │
│   MESSAGE TAKEN BY  .............................         │
│                                                           │
└─────────────────────────────────────────────────────────┘
```

## Phone Play   Student B

You are Mrs Taylor's assistant. Mrs Taylor is at the restaurant. She is coming back at 3 o'clock.

# Listening Practice

*1*  Write the phone numbers from the tape.

1  ......................................... 4  .........................................

2  ......................................... 5  .........................................

3  .........................................

*2*  Write the month and year from the tape.

1  ......................................... 4  .........................................

2  ......................................... 5  .........................................

3  .........................................

*3*  Write the letters.

1  ......................................... 4  .........................................

2  ......................................... 5  .........................................

3  .........................................

*4*  Write the times you hear.

1  ......................................... 4  .........................................

2  ......................................... 5  .........................................

3  .........................................

## *Phone Play   Student A*

Call Student B. Your name is Mr Bradburn. You want to confirm your appointment tomorrow with Miss Wells.

# Getting the Message

Listen to the message on tape and note down the important information.

```
┌────────────────────────────────────────────────────┐
│                                                    │
│   TO ........................  DATE ............... │
│   FROM .....................   TIME ............... │
│                                                    │
│   MESSAGE                                          │
│                                                    │
│   ................................................ │
│   ................................................ │
│   ................................................ │
│   ................................................ │
│   ................................................ │
│   ................................................ │
│   ................................................ │
│                                                    │
│   MESSAGE TAKEN BY ............................... │
│                                                    │
└────────────────────────────────────────────────────┘
```

## *Phone Play   Student B*

You are Miss Well's colleague. Miss Wells is ill. Her appointments are cancelled this week.

# Listening Practice

**1**   Write the numbers you hear on the tape:

1 ................................................   4 ................................................

2 ................................................   5 ................................................

3 ................................................

**2**   What time is it?

1 ................................................   4 ................................................

2 ................................................   5 ................................................

3 ................................................

**3**   Write the telephone numbers you hear.

1 ................................................   4 ................................................

2 ................................................   5 ................................................

3 ................................................

**4**   Underline the stress in each sentence. Then practise saying them yourself.

1  Hold the line, please.          3  Can I help you?

2  Who's speaking, please?          4  He's at a meeting.

## *Phone Play   Student A*

Call Student B. You are Mr Kostalas. Ask for Mr Dioso. You want to meet him tomorrow. You are busy on Thursday. Today is Tuesday.

# Getting the Message

Listen to the message on the tape and note down the important information.

TO ............................... DATE ...................

FROM ............................. TIME ...................

MESSAGE

.................................................................

.................................................................

.................................................................

.................................................................

.................................................................

.................................................................

.................................................................

MESSAGE TAKEN BY ...........................................

## *Phone Play    Student B*

You are Mr Dioso. You have a meeting tomorrow, but you are free on Thursday and Friday. Today is Tuesday.

# **L**istening Practice

*1*  Write the telephone numbers you hear.

1  .................................................... 4  ....................................................

2  .................................................... 5  ....................................................

3  ....................................................

*2*  Circle the correct letters.

1  BI    BA    BE    BY        4  JE    GE    JI    GI

2  HY    HI    AE    AI        5  BB    BV    VB    VV

3  AM    EM    IM    OM

*3*  Make a note of the times.

1  .................................................... 4  ....................................................

2  .................................................... 5  ....................................................

3  ....................................................

*4*  Punctuation. Listen carefully and write exactly what you hear.

1  .................................................... 4  ....................................................

2  .................................................... 5  ....................................................

3  ....................................................

---

## *Phone Play   Student A*

**Call the Channel Travel Service. You want to book a ferry from Dover to Calais on Wednesday 12th at 8am for your boss.**

# Getting the Message

Listen to the message on tape and note down the important information.

TO ................................. DATE ........................

FROM ............................ TIME ........................

MESSAGE

.................................................................................

.................................................................................

.................................................................................

.................................................................................

.................................................................................

.................................................................................

.................................................................................

MESSAGE TAKEN BY ........................................

## Phone Play   Student B

You work for the Channel Travel Service. (Give the name of your company when you answer.) The morning ferries from Dover to Calais leave at 6am, 7am and 9am. Ferries from Folkestone to Calais leave at 8am and 10am.

# ■ *unit 20a* ■
# **L**istening Practice

*1*   Write the phone numbers on tape.

1 ..................................................   4 ..................................................

2 ..................................................   5 ..................................................

3 ..................................................

*2*   Write the numbers you hear.

1 ..................................................   4 ..................................................

2 ..................................................   5 ..................................................

3 ..................................................

*3*   Circle the right number.

1  101    110    111      4  616    660    666

2  218    280    880      5  719    790    729

3  333    303    323

*4*   Write down the address in the USA from the tape.

..................................................................................

..................................................................................

..................................................................................

..................................................................................

## *Phone Play*  *Student A*

You are Mr Lewis of Imperial Motors Ltd. Call Mr Takenashe. You can't go to the sales meeting on 5th June in Tokyo. You are on holiday in July.

# Getting the Message

Listen to the message on tape and note down the important information.

| | | |
|---|---|---|
| To ......................................... | Date ......................... | |
| From ................................. | Time ......................... | |

MESSAGE

.........................................................................................................

.........................................................................................................

.........................................................................................................

.........................................................................................................

.........................................................................................................

.........................................................................................................

.........................................................................................................

MESSAGE TAKEN BY .............................................

---

## *Phone Play   Student B*

You are Mr Takenashe's colleague. Mr Takenashe is in hospital. The meeting is postponed to 10th July.

# Listening Practice

*1*  Write the names of the cities on the tape.

1 ...................................................... 4 ......................................................

2 ...................................................... 5 ......................................................

3 ......................................................

*2*  Make a note of the times you hear.

1 ...................................................... 4 ......................................................

2 ...................................................... 5 ......................................................

3 ......................................................

*3*  Write the dates on tape.

1 ...................................................... 4 ......................................................

2 ...................................................... 5 ......................................................

3 ......................................................

*4*  Circle the correct group of letters.

1 WVU   VWY   YWV   UVW        3 GYJ   JGJ   YJG   IYG

2 HAE   EIH   HAI   IEA          4 VVB   DBV   BBB   BVV

## Phone Play   Student A

Call the New Yorker Hotel. Book a double room for 3 nights from 9th to 12th May. You have a baby. Ask for prices and book.

Listen to the message on tape and note down the important information.

---

To .................................... Date .......................

From .................................... Time .......................

MESSAGE

....................................................................

....................................................................

....................................................................

....................................................................

....................................................................

....................................................................

....................................................................

MESSAGE TAKEN BY ....................................

---

## *Phone Play   Student B*

You are the receptionist at the New Yorker Hotel. A single room costs $110, a double room costs $150, dogs and children are free. Ask for Student A's name.

# Listening Practice

*1*  Write the dates you hear.

1 ............................................  4 ..............................................

2 ............................................  5 ..............................................

3 ............................................

*2*  Write the letters from the tape.

1 ............................................  4 ..............................................

2 ............................................  5 ..............................................

3 ............................................

*3*  Circle the correct time.

1  7.15   19.15          4  3.15   3.50

2  8.40   8.14           5  5.15   4.45

3  1.50   2.10

*4*  Make a note of the address in Sweden from the tape.

..................................................................

..................................................................

..................................................................

..................................................................

## Phone Play   Student A

You work for the Office Paper Shop. Phone Mr Pitts at Paper Suppliers Ltd to place an urgent order for 8000 white window envelopes.

# Getting the Message

Listen to the message on tape and note down the important information.

TO ............................................ DATE ........................

FROM ........................................ TIME ........................

MESSAGE

............................................................................................

............................................................................................

............................................................................................

............................................................................................

............................................................................................

............................................................................................

............................................................................................

MESSAGE TAKEN BY ............................................................

## *Phone Play   Student B*

You work for Paper Suppliers Ltd. You are Mr Pitts' colleague. Mr Pitts is on holiday for 2 weeks. You sell envelopes. Orders under 10,000 – no discount. Orders over 10,000 – you give 10% discount.

# Listening Practice

*1*    Write the phone numbers you hear.

1 ............................................    4 ............................................

2 ............................................    5 ............................................

3 ............................................

*2*    Write the names of these countries.

1 ............................................    4 ............................................

2 ............................................    5 ............................................

3 ............................................

*3*    Circle the correct date.

1   3/9/90     3/9/91        4   21/3/73    31/3/73

2   17/6/89    17/7/89      5   20/8/84    31/12/99

3   14/10/92   4/10/92

*4*    Take down the Greek address from the tape.

............................................................

............................................................

............................................................

............................................................

## Phone Play   Student A

Call Jeff Morris. Give your name. You can't go to the restaurant with him today. You want to invite him tomorrow.

# Getting the Message

Listen to the message on tape and note down the important information.

TO ............................................. DATE ........................

FROM ................................. TIME ........................

MESSAGE

.......................................................................................

.......................................................................................

.......................................................................................

.......................................................................................

.......................................................................................

.......................................................................................

.......................................................................................

MESSAGE TAKEN BY ...............................................

## Phone Play   Student B

You are Jeff Morris's secretary. Mr Morris is out all morning. You don't know where he is. He's going directly to the Gourmand Restaurant at 12.30.

# Listening Practice

*1*　Write down the times.

1　.................................................　4　.................................................

2　.................................................　5　.................................................

3　.................................................

*2*　Make a note of the names of these airports on tape.

1　.................................................　4　.................................................

2　.................................................　5　.................................................

3　.................................................

*3*　Underline the stress in each sentence. Then practise saying them yourself.

1　He's abroad this week.　　　3　The meeting's cancelled.

2　Can he call you back at　　　4　What's your address, please?
　　five o'clock?

*4*　Write these special dates. What are their names?

1　.................................................　4　.................................................

2　.................................................　5　.................................................

3　.................................................

---

## *Phone Play   Student A*

Call Double Peaks Travel. You are Mr Todd. Change your flight from New York to Seattle from 21st October to 22nd October. You have an economy class ticket.

# Getting the Message

Listen to the message on tape and note down the important information.

To ................................... Date ......................

From ................................ Time ........................

MESSAGE

...........................................................................

...........................................................................

...........................................................................

...........................................................................

...........................................................................

...........................................................................

...........................................................................

MESSAGE TAKEN BY ............................................

---

## Phone Play   Student B

You work at Double Peaks Travel. Economy Class is full on all flights
from New York to Seattle from 22nd to 25th October. Suggest Business
Class on the 22nd. (There is a seat in Economy on the 21st but it is on
the late flight, leaving at 23.00.)

# Listening Practice

*1*   Write down the first names you hear on tape.

1 .................................................   4 .................................................

2 .................................................   5 .................................................

3 .................................................


*2*   Write the phone numbers you hear.

1 .................................................   4 .................................................

2 .................................................   5 .................................................

3 .................................................


*3*   Make a note of the times you hear.

1 .................................................   4 .................................................

2 .................................................   5 .................................................

3 .................................................


*4*   Write down the Brazilian address. Make sure you write it correctly.

.................................................................................

.................................................................................

.................................................................................

.................................................................................


## *Phone Play   Student A*

Call FASG Chemicals. Your name is Graham Drake. You work for Agri Pro. Ask for the Technical Manager of FASG. You want some information on new phosphate products.

# Getting the Message

Listen to the message on tape and note down the important information.

```
┌─────────────────────────────────────────────────────────┐
│                                                         │
│   TO  .........................   DATE ................ │
│   FROM .........................  TIME ................ │
│                                                         │
│                                                         │
│   MESSAGE                                               │
│                                                         │
│   ..................................................... │
│                                                         │
│   ..................................................... │
│                                                         │
│   ..................................................... │
│                                                         │
│   ..................................................... │
│                                                         │
│   ..................................................... │
│                                                         │
│   ..................................................... │
│                                                         │
│   ..................................................... │
│                                                         │
│   MESSAGE TAKEN BY  ................................... │
│                                                         │
└─────────────────────────────────────────────────────────┘
```

## *Phone Play   Student B*

You work for FASG Chemicals. The Technical Manager is in South America this week. Suggest a presentation on new phosphates developments at FASG. Fix a date and time. Ask for Student A's name and the name of his company.

# Listening Practice

*1*    Write the names of the cities on the tape.

1 ................................................    4 ................................................

2 ................................................    5 ................................................

3 ................................................

*2*    Write the dates you hear on tape.

1 ................................................    4 ................................................

2 ................................................    5 ................................................

3 ................................................

*3*    Circle the correct time.

| | | | | | | |
|---|---|---|---|---|---|---|
| 1 | 13.30 | 2.30 | | 4 | 2.15 | 1.45 |
| 2 | 2pm | 2am | | 5 | 9.30 | 19.30 |
| 3 | 10.15 | 9.45 | | | | |

*4*    Make a note of the German address on tape.

................................................................

................................................................

................................................................

................................................................

................................................................

## Phone Play   Student A

You want to buy a Cox Word Processor for your office. Call Cox Office Machines and ask for the Sales Department. Ask about price, delivery, discounts, etc.

# Getting the Message

Listen to the message on tape and note down the important information.

---

TO ............................... DATE .....................

FROM ................................ TIME ........................

MESSAGE

........................................................................

........................................................................

........................................................................

........................................................................

........................................................................

........................................................................

........................................................................

MESSAGE TAKEN BY ...............................................

---

## *Phone Play   Student B*

You work for Cox Office Machines. Invite Student A for a demonstration.
Fix date, time, etc and take his name and the name of his company.

# Listening Practice

*1*  Write the numbers you hear on tape.

1  ....................................................  4  ....................................................

2  ....................................................  5  ....................................................

3  ....................................................

*2*  Write the surnames you hear on tape.

1  ....................................................  4  ....................................................

2  ....................................................  5  ....................................................

3  ....................................................

*3*  Circle the dates you hear on tape.

1  30/8/92    31/8/82  4  April 26th    April 25th

2  30th May    13th May  5  31st March    31st May

3  6th March    16th March

*4*  Underline the strong stress in each sentence. Practise saying them yourself.

1  I'll put you through.  3  I'm afraid he's out all afternoon.

2  I'd like to speak to Mr Imari, please.  4  What time will he be free?

---

## Phone Play   Student A

Call Mrs Cupp at Peer Potteries. You have just received order no. BC/56. You ordered 24 dinner services, but 18 were delivered. There are 24 on the invoice.

# Getting the Message

Listen to the message on tape and note down the important information.

---

TO ................................................ DATE ........................

FROM ............................................ TIME ........................

MESSAGE

................................................................................

................................................................................

................................................................................

................................................................................

................................................................................

................................................................................

................................................................................

MESSAGE TAKEN BY ................................................

---

## *Phone Play   Student B*

You are Mrs Cupp's secretary at Peer Potteries. Mrs Cupp is abroad this week. Listen to Student A's problem and suggest a solution (change invoice, complete order. . . .)

# Listening Practice

*1*   Circle the number you hear on the tape.

    1  2,894    2,844              4  13,000   30,000

    2  26,808   26,008          5  6,142    6,642

    3  17,659   70,659

*2*   Write the dates you hear.

    1 ................................................    4 ................................................

    2 ................................................    5 ................................................

    3 ................................................

*3*   Make a note of the times you hear.

    1 ................................................    4 ................................................

    2 ................................................    5 ................................................

    3 ................................................

*4*   Write down the Japanese address on tape.

................................................................

................................................................

................................................................

................................................................

---

## *Phone Play   Student A*

You are Mr Biggs, owner of the Perfume Shop. Call Rucci Beauty
Products and ask for Mr Rucci. You can't pay invoice no. 66329 of
$1,550 for the moment. Invent a good reason!

# Getting the Message

Listen to the message on tape and note down the important information.

```
┌─────────────────────────────────────────────────────┐
│                                                       │
│   TO  ...........................  DATE ............   │
│   FROM .........................  TIME ............    │
│                                                       │
│   MESSAGE                                             │
│                                                       │
│   ..................................................  │
│   ..................................................  │
│   ..................................................  │
│   ..................................................  │
│   ..................................................  │
│   ..................................................  │
│   ..................................................  │
│                                                       │
│   MESSAGE TAKEN BY  ...............................   │
│                                                       │
└─────────────────────────────────────────────────────┘
```

## *Phone Play   Student B*

You work for Rucci Beauty Products. Mr Rucci is busy and can't be disturbed. Try and help Student A, (who is always a bad customer).

# key
# Answers to all Exercises

This Key contains the answers to all the exercises and the full text of all recorded material which is not in the student's unit.
In exercises where there is more than one answer, we have given suggestions.

## Unit 1

*2*  **1** – D  **2** – A  **3** – E  **4** – C  **5** – B

*4*  **a**  Interface. Good morning. Can I help you?
Hello. Can I speak to Mr Stevenson, please?
One moment, please. I'm putting you through.

**b**  PLC International. Good afternoon.
I'd like to speak to Mr Davies, please.
Who's speaking, please?
This is Charles Windsor of Micro Logics.
Hold the line, please. I'll connect you.

*5*  Good morning. Belfry Consultants.
Can I speak to Mr Brown, please?
Can I have your name, please? (Who's calling?)
Brian Howard of Jason's.
Hold the line, Mr Howard.
I'll put you through.

## Unit 2

*2*  **1** – C  **2** – H  **3** – F  **4** – A  **5** – I  **6** – E  **7** – B  **8** – D  **9** – G

*3*  **a**  I'm afraid Mr Jones is at a meeting.
Oh dear. What time will he be free?
At about 4 o'clock.
Well, could you take a message, please?

**b**  Hello. I'm sorry but Gloria is on another line.
Can I help you?
No, that's all right. Could you just tell her I called.

*4*    Good morning. Jose Vidal speaking.
I'd like to speak to Mrs Rossi, please.
I'm sorry, but Mrs Rossi is out at the moment. Can you call back later?
What time will she be back?
In about 20 minutes.
Thank you.
You're welcome. Goodbye.

*5*    **1** He won't be back till Thursday.
**2** We open again on Tuesday morning.
**3** We shall be closed from Monday the 16th until Wednesday the 18th.
**4** The best time to ring is before lunch on Fridays or after 5pm on Mondays.

*6*    **1** 16th   **2** 17th   **3** 15th   **4** 23rd   **5** 24th   **6** 9th   **7** 31st

# Unit 3

*2*    **1** – A   **2** – C   **3** – E   **4** – B   **5** – D

*3*    Suggestions: **a** No, this is (LTP). **b** I'm sorry there's nobody of that name
here. (there's no Miss Van Hertzen here.) **c** No, this is . . . .

*4*    Susan McQueen speaking. Good afternoon.
Is that extension 584?
No, this is 554 . . . I'll put you back to the switchboard.
Thanks for your help.
That's all right. Goodbye.

*5*    **1** Good afternoon. Can I speak to Patricia Smith, please?
> I'm sorry there's nobody of that name here. My name's Dorothy
Smith.

**2** Is that 992 4897?
> I'm afraid you've got the wrong number. This is 992 4097.

**3** Good morning. I'd like to speak to Mr Thomson, please.
> I'm sorry there's no Mr Thomson here.

*6*    **1** – A   **2** – H   **3** – G   **4** – B   **5** – E   **6** – D   **7** – C   **8** – F

# Unit 4

### 3

This is Paul Down speaking.
Pardon?
Paul Down speaking.
Sorry, but the line is very bad.
Paul Down.
Could you spell that, please?
P..A..U..L...D..O..W..N.
Could you repeat that, please?
P..A..U..L...D..O..W..N.
Sorry, but I still don't understand.
P..A..U.....
Ah, Good afternoon, Mr Down. How are you?

### 4

**1** pardon   **2** slowly   **3** understand   **4** still   **5** up

**6** repeat   **7** English   **8** line   **9** confirm

# Unit 5

### 3

Suggestions: **1** This is .......... I'm sorry I'm not available at the moment. Please ring back tomorrow.   **2** .......... I'm sorry but our office is closed for the day. We are open from .......... to .......... , Monday to Friday. Please call back tomorrow. **3** .......... The office has closed for today. Please call again tomorrow after 9 am. Thank you for calling.

### 4

**1** This is LTP. Please hold the line. We're sorry to keep you waiting.

**2** This is Henry Barber's office. I'm not free right now, but if you leave me your name and your phone number, I'll call you back when I return. Please speak after the tone.

# Unit 6

### 3

**1** fifty one   **2** eight hundred and twelve   **3** four thousand, seven hundred and thirty nine   **4** two hundred and four thousand, one hundred and ten

### 4

**1** 28,914   **2** 704   **3** 2,351   **4** 634,405

**5**  **Across** **1** – 232   **3** – 3084   **5** – 94   **6** – 40968   **10** – 45089   **11** – 23
**13** – 2690   **14** – 513

**Down** **1** – 219914   **2** – 27   **3** – 3102   **4** – 8765   **7** – 824363
**8** – 7516   **9** – 4860   **12** – 75

# Unit 7

**2**  **1** – 041 456 9567   **2** – 22 39 29 02   **3** – 69 60 51 233   **4** – 236 42 84

**3**  Brown – 47681       Bunter – 12244    Carlsson – 98805
Davidson – 02036   Ford – 11503     Hindley – 90410

**4**  Amsterdam 20 67 02 22          Brussels 2 514 67 00
Copenhagen 1 56 48 66          Dublin 1 51 88 44
Frankfurt 69 80 455            Helsinki 0 356 081

# Unit 8

**2**  Curie 1867         Marx 1893        Greene 1904
Kennedy 1917       Kelly 1928       Edward 1964

**4**  **1** 30th – wrong      **2** 31st – correct    **3** 10th – wrong
**4** 19th – wrong      **5** 5th – wrong       **6** 11th – correct

**6**  **1** 8/6/94   **2** 9/16/94   **3** 11/10/1963   **4** 7/31/1939
**5** the sixth of August, nineteen ninety one
**6** June eighth, nineteen ninety one
**7** the twentieth of October, nineteen ninety four
**8** December fourteenth, nineteen ninety six

**7**  Now, I mustn't forget to pick up John Sanderson from the airport on the
19th. I'm having lunch with Margo on the 22nd and I have to confirm the
I.R.T. Sales Representative's hotel on the 24th. Oh yes, they're coming to
install the new photocopier on the 20th and I must remember my dentist's
appointment on the 21st.

# Unit 9

**3**  **1** five past twelve     **2** twenty five past two
**3** twenty to eleven     **4** five to eleven

**4**  **1** 20.45 or 8.45pm     **2** 10.10 or 10.10am
**3** 0.55 or 0.55am       **4** 23.25 or 11.25pm

**5**    Welcome to the Rex Cinema. Here are the times of our films this week:
In Cinema 1 you can see Mad Max 11 showing at 14.00, 16.35, 19.25 and 22.00.
In Cinema 2 there is Rocky 15 showing at 13.30, 16.15, 19.00, 21.45.
In Cinema 3 the film is Terminator 7 showing at 13.50, 16.30, 19.10 and 21.50.
In Cinema 4 we have Rambo XX showing at 13.35, 16.15, 18.55 and 21.35.
And finally, in Cinema 5 there is Henry V showing at 13.15, 16.35 and 19.55.

## Unit 10

**4**    Suggestions: Apple, Book, Cat, Dog, Elephant, France, Germany, Hello, India, Japan, King, Lion, Macdonalds, North, Orange, Peter, Queen, Rat, Snow, Think, Under, Victory, William, X-ray, Yes, Zebra.

**5**    **1**   Family name: HACKWORTH: Forenames: LARRY BEVAN
Place of birth: PHOENIX, USA

      **2**   Family name: VILLARD: Forename: ANTOINE
Place of birth: TOULOUSE, FRANCE

      **3**   Family name: SCHEELER: Forenames: MONIKA JUTTA
Place of birth: STEYR, AUSTRIA

      **4**   Family name: KIDANE: Forename: ABEBA
Place of birth: HARRAR, ETHIOPIA

## Unit 11

**4**    **1**   Workwell Watches' new address is:
WEINPLATZ 8/9
8002 ZURICH

      **2**   The Goya Art Gallery is moving to:
Calle de General Oraa 68
28006 MADRID

      **3**   Pyramid Sandpaper Ltd's new address is:
49 GAWAD HOSNI STREET
PO BOX 464
CAIRO

## Unit 12

**2**  **1** on the 18th June   **2** at two o'clock   **3** on Wednesday
**4** in the afternoon   **5** on December the 25th (on Christmas Day)
**6** at night

**4**  **1** at   **2** at   **3** on   **4** on   **5** at (in)   **6** in

**5**  **1** Please ask Mr Smith to meet me at Victoria Station on 3rd May at 11 o'clock.
**2** Terry is in Mexico on a business trip at the silver factory this week.
**3** Our phone rings more in the morning than in the afternoon and never in the evening.
**4** I'll be in my office or at the conference on Wednesday when you arrive.
**5** The company will be closed in August and at Christmas.
**6** I'm coming to Tokyo on Friday and staying until Tuesday.
**7** Please finish this project by the end of the month.
**8** Mr Brown's secretary is going to the bank before she goes home.

(NOTE: no preposition in the last example.)

**6**  **1** at   **2** in   **3** on   **4** at

## Unit 13

**1**  **a** Could I speak to Mr Davidson, please.
Certainly. Could I have your name, please?
Hold the line, Mr Schwarz.

**b** I'm sorry Mr Davidson is on holiday this week. Would you like to leave a message?
Could you spell that, please.
It's S..U..double S..M..A..N.

**c** Hold on, please. I'll put you back to the switchboard.

**2**  **1** – G   **2** – F   **3** – I   **4** – J   **5** – H
**6** – A   **7** – B   **8** – D   **9** – E   **10** – C

**3**  international code . . . area code

**4**  **1** Thank you for calling Godfrey Smith Associates. I'm sorry there's nobody (no one) here to answer your call. If you leave your name and telephone number after the tone, we'll ring you back as soon as we can.

**2** CPA Ltd. All lines are engaged at present. Your call is in a queue. Please hold on and your call will be answered shortly.

**3** Mediterranean Tours. Our office is now closed for the day. Our office hours are from 9.30 am till 5.30 pm. If you would like us to call you back, please leave your name and number after the tone.

**5**  1 – D  2 – F  3 – A  4 – H  5 – B  6 – G  7 – E  8 – C

**6**  . . . . that's capital K..capital K..5 stroke... capital B..capital A..capital F..new line..two..oh..five..Bradford Road... new line.. Bingley..I'll spell that..B..I..N..G..L..E..Y..new line and then the postal code is BD..97...5..PF.

**7**

| | | |
|---|---|---|
| **1** please | **2** calling (speaking) | **3** moment |
| **4** through | **5** message | **6** called |
| **7** that name here | **8** bothered you | **9** wrong number |
| **10** fax | **11** bad | **12** up |
| **13** more slowly | **14** tone | |

**8**

| | | | | | | |
|---|---|---|---|---|---|---|
| **1** in | **2** in | **3** in | **4** at | **5** on | **6** on | **7** on |
| **8** in at | **9** at | **10** on | **11** after | **12** at | **13** on | **14** from to |
| **15** on | **16** on | **17** on | **18** at | **19** at | **20** for | |

# Unit 14A

**1**  1 – 5420  2 – 9647  3 – 7129  4 – 1584  5 – 6710

**2**  1 – BCST  2 – FWXM  3 – ZYHB  4 – LOQD  5 – JKPU

**3**  1 – BA 804  2 – AF 322  3 – TW 209  4 – SA 674  5 – PA 002

**4**  1 - CBAO  2 – JAXW  3 – FEIP  4 – YIVM  5 – SAJG

# Unit 14 B

**Message:** To Mr Lee from Mr Black. He'll call back at 5 o'clock today.

**Script:** Hello. It's 10 o'clock on Friday 4th. This is Mr Black. Black..B..L..A..C..K. I wanted to speak to Mr Lee. L..E..E. Well, I'll call him back at 5pm. Yes, 5 o'clock this afternoon.

# Unit 15A

**1**  1 – 72 84 91  2 – 63 56 33  3 – 96 55 48  4 – 80 12 17  5 – 53 81 27

**2**  1 – G  2 – C  3 – Q  4 – S  5 – Z

**3**  1 – 1992  2 – 1990  3 – 1979  4 – 1984  5 – 1909

**4**  1 34/AV-Z  2 QS.216-3  3 DH 45 F4

## Unit 15B

**Message:** To Mary from Bill. Call Bill back at 11 o'clock tomorrow. Tel – 01 692 3478.

**Script:** Hello, Mary. This is Bill. It's 9 o'clock on Friday. Could you call me back at 11 o'clock. My number is 01 692 3478. 01 692 3478. Thank you.

## Unit 16A

*1*   **1** – EAIE     **2** – JIEJ     **3** – HAYV     **4** – AEBI     **5** – IVAG

*2*   **1** – 70 15 80   **2** – 18 50 15   **3** – 16 14 13   **4** – 90 19 18   **5** – 20 12 70

*3*   **1** – B     **2** – I     **3** – Y     **4** – G     **5** – H

*4*   **1** – 80     **2** – 17     **3** – 16     **4** – 15     **5** – 30

## Unit 16B

**Message:** To Mr Jackson from Mrs Cooper. Coming to meeting at 9.30 on Friday. Send her BIO 92 Doc by fax.

**Script:** Good afternoon. It's Monday 7th at 12.15. Could you give a message to Mr Jackson. Jackson, J..A..C..K..S..O..N. This is Mrs Cooper, C..O..O..P..E..R. I just wanted to confirm that I'll be coming to the meeting on Friday at 9.30. Please could you send me the BIO 92 documentation by fax. BIO 92. Thanks.

## Unit 17A

*1*   **1** – 2 482 91 19     **2** – 222 19 84 36     **3** – 051 586 2133
      **4** – 5 699 910       **5** – 23691

*2*   **1**  July 1989         **2**  August 1991        **3**  March 1984
      **4**  February 1988     **5**  October 1994

*3*   **1**  BU JA SI          **2**  KL MN FS           **3**  VI BR AO
      **4**  JE GA IY          **5**  TB PL SM

*4*   **1**  8.15              **2**  9.30               **3**  7.40
      **4**  20.50             **5**  22.10

## Unit 17B

**Message:** To Bob Castaneda from Sylvia Conway. Meet her at Henry's Bar this evening at 8 o'clock. Call back on 249 68 34 to confirm.

**Script:** Hi! Today's Saturday. The time is 8.30 in the morning. This is Sylvia Conway. Sylvia Conway, C..O..N..W..A..Y. Could you tell Bob Castaneda C..A..S..T..A..N..E..D..A to meet me at Henry's Bar, Henry's Bar this evening at 8. O.K? 8 o'clock at Henry's Bar. Would you ask him to call me back to confirm? My number is 249 68 34. 249 68 34. Thanks.

## Unit 18A

*1*
| | | | | | | | | | |
|---|---|---|---|---|---|---|---|---|---|
| **1** | 7th | 4th | 12th | **2** | 14th | 22nd | 23rd | **3** | 11th 15th 6th |
| **4** | 9th | 30th | 28th | **5** | 1st | 13th | 19th | | |

*2*
| **1** 16.30 | **2** 10.45 | **3** 3.30 | **4** 17.15 | **5** 9.30 |
|---|---|---|---|---|

*3*
| **1** 80 90 314 | **2** 18 19 340 | **3** 21 39 481 |
|---|---|---|
| **4** 622 411 512 | **5** 17 35 206 | |

*4*
1 Hold the <u>line</u>, please.  
2 Who's <u>speak</u>ing, please?  
3 Can I <u>help</u> you?  
4 He's at a <u>meet</u>ing.

## Unit 18B

**Message:** To Mrs Pandros from Mr Strasser. Send doc numbers 382A and 382B by fax. Conference in Athens on 18 December.

**Script:** Good morning. It's Tuesday evening – 7 pm. My name is Mr. Strasser. Strasser, S..T..R..A..S..S..E..R. I have a message for Mrs Pandros, P..A..N..D..R..O..S. I need the following documentation: Could you ask her to send me doc numbers 382A and 382B by fax. I repeat. 382A and 382B. Could you also tell her that I have organised a conference in Athens for the 18th of December. December 18th in Athens. Goodbye.

## Unit 19A

*1*
| **1** 341 952 84 | **2** 201 495 67 | **3** 12 18 980 |
|---|---|---|
| **4** 605 210 313 | **5** 21 29 209 | |

*2*
| **1** BE | **2** HI | **3** EM | **4** GI | **5** VB |
|---|---|---|---|---|

*3*
| **1** 9.30 | **2** 2.45 | **3** 15.15 | **4** 23.30 | **5** 11.45 |
|---|---|---|---|---|

*4*
| **1** 458/RT – AZ | **2** DC20 WX/E | **3** 2 4 6 SCV – 15 |
|---|---|---|
| **4** D.B.N. 24/D | **5** 67332 ASED.3 | |

## Unit 19B

**Message:** To Mrs Henderson from Mr McCall. Coming to New York 7th May. Flight number TW670. Arrive 16.40 Kennedy Airport.

**Script:** Hello. It's the 1st of May at 11 am UK time. I'm Mr. McCall and I have a message for Mrs Henderson. McCall M..c..C..A..L..L and the message is for Mrs Henderson H..E..N..D..E..R..S..O..N. Could you tell her that I'm coming to New York on the 7th of May. Yes, the 7th. I'll be arriving on Flight Number TW670, TW670 at 20 to 5, that's 16.40 at Kennedy Airport. Many thanks.

## Unit 20A

**1**
1 2246 91 00    2 3 314 09 22    3 21 864 15 73
4 81 90 00    5 592 40 68

**2**
1 30th  31st  13th    2 11th  3rd  5th    3 17th  14th  21st
4 20th  9th  23rd    5 22nd 16th  18th

**3**
1 110    2 280    3 323    4 616    5 790

**4**
Pot Garage
101 Newbury Street
Palm Beach
Florida 33480

## Unit 20B

**Message:** To Mr Dupont from Miss Baker. Arriving Paris on September 9th, 15.40 CDG airport. Meet her. Confirm by next Monday.

**Script:** Hi! I'm Miss Baker calling from New York. It's August 25th at 4 o'clock my time. My name is Baker, B..A..K..E..R. Could you give a message to Mr DuPont. Please tell him that I'll be arriving in Paris on the September 10th. No, sorry the 9th of September at 20 to 4 in the afternoon. Got it? The September 9th at 15.40 at CDG Airport. Could you ask him to meet me there? And to confirm by next Monday. Thanks. Bye.

## Unit 21A

**1**
1 Vienna    2 Warsaw    3 Paris    4 Berlin    5 Brussels

**2**
1 14.00    2 6.30    3 19.20    4 15.15    5 9.25

**3**
1 8th September    2 19th March    3 22nd June
4 30th May    5 13th January

**4**
1 YWV    2 IEA    3 GYJ    4 BVV

## Unit 21B

**Message:** To Mr Oshemazi from Caroline Barry. Invitation to lunch. Not free Monday or Thursday next week. Call by 5.30 this afternoon. Telephone 061 982 2200 or at home – 061 977 8101 this evening.

**Script:** Hello. It's Thursday at 12.30. This is Caroline Barry. B..A..double R..Y. I want to invite Mr Oshemazi, Mr Oshemazi O..S..H..E..M..A..Z..I to lunch next week. I'm free on Monday and Tuesday. Oh no, wait a minute, I'm NOT free on Monday. . . or Thursday, but any other day is fine. Could he call me back before 5.30 this afternoon. My number is 061 982 2200, I repeat, 061 982 2200. Or call me at home this evening on 061 977 8101, 061 977 8101.

## Unit 22A

*1*
  1 The invoice date was 16/1/87.    2 His date of birth is 24/4/35.
  3 The date she started was 28/11/92. 4 The date of the contract is 15/2/93.
  5 It was installed on 7/7/90.

*2*
  1 BIN VEN PAD   2 QST RED RID     3 MNB AJL YWB
  4 AEI GID JYD   5 HOF LDY BVC

*3*
  1 I'm arriving at 19.15.
  2 The plane leaves at 8.40.
  3 The departure time is 2.10.
  4 We'll have to check in by 3.50 at the latest.
  5 Is 4.45 the last appointment?

*4*
My business address is as follows:
Erikssons Tryckeri
Storgatan 13
850 00 Sundsvall
Sweden

## Unit 22B

**Message:** To Malcolm MacDonald from Joseph Evans. Can't come to Glasgow 20th July. Coming 25th to 30th. Change date of meeting from 22nd to 26th.

**Script:** Good afternoon. It's Wednesday 12th at 11.30 in the morning. This is Joseph Evans. I have a message for Malcolm MacDonald. Do you want me to spell those names for you? Evans, E..V..A..N..S for Malcolm MacDonald, M..A..C..capital D..O..N..A..L..D. I can't come to Glasgow on the 20th July. I'm coming on the 25th and staying until the 30th. From the 25th to the 30th. Could you change the dates of my meeting from the 22nd to the 26th. So NO meeting on the 22nd. It's on the 26th.

## Unit 23A

### 1

1 My new number is 071 682 3113.

2 Why not ring me on 391 22 48?

3 His private line is 734 616 91.

4 He's at our Edinburgh office today. The number's 031 440 1867.

5 Let me find the number. Ah, here it is. It's 800 6193.

### 2

1 It's a shipment for Kuwait.

2 The raw materials come from India.

3 The last conference was in Spain.

4 The situation in Russia is uncertain at the moment.

5 The last consignment came from Norway.

### 3

1 The first meeting was on the 3rd of September 1990.

2 The Washington office was opened on the 17th of July 1989.

3 The invoice date is the 4th of October 1992.

4 Her application form says the 21st of March 1973.

5 The contract expires on the 31st December 1999.

### 4

Our Greek agent's address is as follows:
Hellas Holidays
483 Thisseos Street
Kallithea
176 76 Athens

## Unit 23B

**Message:** To Jennifer Buckley from Mr Zetland. Stuck in Mali. Send flowers and card to his wife 18th February. Mrs Jane Zetland, 1879 Sioux Avenue, Salt Lake City, Utah.

**Script:** 11.15 am Monday. I'd like to leave a message for my secretary, Jennifer Buckley. B..U..C..K..L..E..Y. This is Mr Zetland, Z..E..T..L..A..N..D. I'm in Mali and it's my wife's birthday next week on the 18th February, the 18th. Could you ask Jennifer to send her flowers and a card. Here's my wife's name and address: Mrs Jane Zetland, again, Zetland, 1879 Sioux Avenue, 1879 Sioux, S..I..O..U..X Avenue, Salt Lake City, Utah. Thank you, Goodbye.

## Unit 24A

### 1

1 We'll have coffee at half past three.

2 The arrival time is 16.20.

3 Ring and tell them I'll be there at about ten to seven.

4 I'm sorry to say that your flight arrives in Delhi at 2.55 am.

5 They said that you'll arrive at five to three in the morning.

*2*  **1** London Heathrow  **2** Paris Charles de Gaulle  **3** J F Kennedy
**4** Milan Malpensa  **5** Stockholm Arlanda  **6** London Gatwick
**7** Narita Tokyo  **8** Rome Leonardo da Vinci

*3*  **1** He's ab<u>road</u> this week.  **2** Can he call you <u>back</u> at 5 o'clock?
**3** The meeting's <u>cancelled</u>.  **4** What's your ad<u>dress</u>, please?

*4*  **1** 25th of December (Christmas Day).
**2** 4th of July (American Independence Day).
**3** 1st of January (New Year's Day).
**4** 14th of February (St Valentine's Day).
**5** 1st of May (May Day).

# Unit 24B

**Message:** To Al Curtis from Beth Whittle. Meeting on 3rd November from 9.30 to 12.15. Lunch at the Strand Palace Hotel. Meeting from 14.00 to 16.45.

**Script:** 17.15, 1st October. Good morning. This is Beth Whittle, Beth Whittle, W..H..I..T..T..L..E calling with a message for Al Curtis, C..U..R..T..I..S. I want to give you the exact times of the meeting on the 3rd November, the meeting on the 3rd November. It begins at half past 9 and finishes for lunch at quarter past 12. So that's 9.30 to 12.15. Then we have lunch at the Strand Palace Hotel – the Strand Palace – it's very central. The meeting continues in the afternoon from 2 o'clock and finishes at quarter to 5, at quarter to 5. O.K? Bye.

# Unit 25A

*1*  **1** James (Robertson)  **2** Barbara (Lawson)  **3** Mathew (Fleming)
**4** Felicity (Barber)  **5** Jane (Woodfall)

*2*  **1** I think it's 923 684 217.
**2** Their new number is 46 83 56.
**3** 11 15 70. Yes, I'm sure it's 11 15 70.
**4** It's been changed to 90 73 33.
**5** The code is 0273 and the number is 736344.

*3*  **1** The taxi is booked for a quarter to twelve.
**2** 22.10. The timetable definitely said ten past ten.
**3** Your train leaves at 21.50 from the Central Station.
**4** Could you book me a taxi for about 7.35 tomorrow morning.
**5** The President is scheduled to arrive at twenty to ten.

*4*  Why not take my Rio address. It's:
Casa de Miguel
Rua Maria Antonia 369-371
20041 Rio de Janeiro
Brazil

## Unit 25B

**Message:** To Jerry Romano from John Waters. Change order. Not 200 metres of XL cable, but 250 metres of XXL. Call Back 442 91 01.

**Script:** Hi! Tuesday, 1.30 pm. This is John Waters. Waters W..A..T..E..R..S calling for Jerry Romano. R..O..M..A..N..O. I'm really sorry but I want to change my order for cable. Please DON'T send me 200 metres of XL cable, NOT 200 metres of XL. I want 250, 250 metres of XXL. So, please send 250 metres of XXL cable. Could you call me back on 442 91 01. I repeat, 442 91 01.

## Unit 26A

*1*
   **1** Could you find me the code for Seoul, Korea.
   **2** Has that fax come in yet from Hong Kong?
   **3** Our office in Singapore is on the line.
   **4** I have a call for you – Mr Numoto in Tokyo.
   **5** Do you know what the time is in Djakarta?

*2*
   **1** We opened your account on the 1st of March 1991.
   **2** The contract expired on the 1st of February 1989.
   **3** The date of renewal is the 11th of January 1994.
   **4** His birthday is the 2nd of May.
   **5** He died on the 1st September 1992.

*3*
   **1** I make it half past one.
   **2** There's a meeting in the board room at 2pm.
   **3** We'll have a short break at a quarter past ten.
   **4** The quarter to two train gets in too late.
   **5** The meeting must finish by 7.30.

*4*
We've just opened a new office in Berlin. The address is as follows:
Buro Feltz
Engesserstrasse 13
Postfach 9621
1000 Berlin
Germany

## Unit 26B

**Message:** To Mr Hernandez from Miss Cole. Problem on invoice no 4926 dated 31st January. Amount on invoice £8752.50 plus VAT. Should be £8725.00 plus VAT. Correct and send new invoice.

**Script:** February 10th at 2.30. Good afternoon. My name is Miss Cole, C..O..L..E and I'm calling to speak to your Mr Hernandez. There's a problem on your invoice number 4926, that's invoice 4926, dated 30th, no 31st January. The amount on the invoice is £8752.50 plus VAT. There's a mistake and it should read £8725.00 plus VAT. Could you correct the invoice and send us a new one. So, it's invoice 4926 and it should be for £8725.00.

Thank you.

# Unit 27A

*1*
  **1** 22,617  **2** 48,170  **3** 70,001   **4** 42,310    **5** 90,919

*2*
  **1** (John) Coleman   **2** (Berit) Lindholm   **3** (Ewa) Michelson
  **4** (Peter) Cusak   **5** (Antonio) Alvarez

*3*
  **1** Today's date is the 30th of August 1992.
  **2** The documents must be in the post by the 13th of May.
  **3** Could you get me a flight to Budapest on the 6th of March.
  **4** The one-day conference is on April the 26th.
  **5** There will be a celebration on the 31st of May.

*4*
  **1** I'll put you <u>through</u>.    **2** I'd like to speak to Mr Im<u>ari</u>, please.
  **3** I'm afraid he's <u>out</u> all afternoon.  **4** What time will he be <u>free</u>?

# Unit 27B

**Message:** To Mr Morris from Lydia Denham. Can't deliver SBN until March. SBK in stock and can be delivered by Friday. 15% discount to compensate. Call back today 388 04 21, extension 556.

**Script:** Good morning. It's 9.30 on Tuesday 13th. My name is Lydia Denham, that's spelt D..E..N..H..A..M. I'm calling for Mr Morris, M..O..R..R..I..S. Could you give him a message for me please. I'm sorry but we can't deliver the SBN order until March. We have SBK in stock at the moment and can deliver it to you by Friday. If you accept the SBK, we'll offer you 15% discount to compensate. Could you ask Mr Morris to call back today. My number is 388 04 21, extension 556. That's 388 04 21, extension 556.

# Unit 28A

*1*
  **1** The order was for 2,844.
  **2** We counted but there were only 26,008.
  **3** That was 17,659 – not 70.
  **4** The initial order will be for 13,000.
  **5** We can supply 6,142 immediately from stock.

*2*
  **1** Can Mr Welsh make the meeting on July 17th?
  **2** He won't be back in the country till May 7th.
  **3** The contract expires on the 31st of December.
  **4** We're closed for holidays from the 1st August.
  **5** We re-open on August the 21st.

*3*   **1** We're planning on catching the 2.35 to Paris Charles de Gaulle.
**2** That means we'll be arriving about 3.25.
**3** We hope to be back in the hotel by about twenty to seven.
**4** The night train leaves at 22.35.
**5** It's now five past eleven, so let's have a break.

*4*   Here's the address of a good contact in Tokyo:
Nippon Electronics
12-20 Akasaka 7 – Chome
Minato – ku
107 Tokyo

## Unit 28B

**Message:** To Jack Springfield from Tony Waller. Liked sample of films. Wants to place an order. 2 boxes of Y20's, 1 box of Y30's and 1 box of X32's as soon as possible.

**Script:** Hello. It's 9.30 pm on Wednesday 25th. This is Tony Waller, that's Waller, W..A..L..L..E..R. I'd like to speak to Jack Springfield or leave him a message. Jack Springfield, S..P..R..I..N..G..F..I..E..L..D. I liked the samples he sent me and I'd like to place an order. Please send me 2 boxes of Y20 films, 1 box of Y30 films and 1 box of X32 films. I'll repeat that. 2 boxes of Y20, 1 box of Y30 and 1 box of X32 films. Oh, and I need them as soon as possible. Thank you.